SOUTH PARK CITY
COLORADO

Photographs by Frank A. Cechner

*In Cooperation with the
South Park Historical Foundation, Inc.*

Photographers of the West Publishers

Acknowledgments

I would like to thank the South Park Historical Foundation, Inc. for their assistance and cooperation. Their dedication to the preservation of a latter 19th century Colorado mining town and the many artifacts, furnished mainly through the generosity of Park County residents, many of whom are the descendents of the early settlers, made this collection of photographs possible.

The South Park City Museum is administered by a non-profit corporation. Admissions and donations are used for the restoration and maintenance of exhibits and buildings. The museum is open every day from May 15th to October 15th. Information may be obtained by calling the Museum office at (303) 836-2387, Fairplay, Colorado.

Frank A. Cechner

Copyright 1987 Frank A. Cechner
All rights reserved.

Library of Congress Number: 87-061171

First Edition

1 2 3 4 5 6 7 8 9

Printed in the United States of America

Design / Typography —
  Richard M. Kohen, Shadow Canyon Graphics

Introduction

South Park is a broad valley in the center of Colorado, at an elevation of 8,500 feet covering over 900 square miles. It is surrounded by the Mosquito and Park ranges with many mountain peaks rising more than 14,000 feet above sea level. The valley, lush with vegetation, is supplied by water from the Middle and South forks of the South Platte River.

The valley supported huge herds of game and colonies of smaller animals such as beaver, muskrat, otter and bobcat. In the midst of this bounty, the Ute Indian made his summer camp and successfully battled the Cheyenne, Arapahoe and Comanche for exclusive possession of his domain.

Colorado was explored in the late 16th and early 17th centuries by the French and Spanish, who established outposts for the purpose of trade with the Indians. The Americanized name of South Park was derived from "parc," the French word for game preserve.

In 1803, the United States acquired the vast wilderness of Colorado as a part of the Louisiana Purchase. Zebulon Pike was dispatched by President Jefferson in 1806 to explore the new territory. In an attempt to map the area, Pike's party penetrated South Park, but only marginally. Finding evidence in the form of fresh campsites that Spanish troops were still in the area, they elected to track the offenders and drifted further and further south, only to be captured in the San Luis Valley and taken to Santa Fe.

Following Pike's release and return to the United States, reports of his explorations and the abundance of game drew the attention of hunters and trappers. Fur trading became the first economic endeavor of the period, and was followed in the mid-19th century by the development of cattle and sheep ranching. The first ditch rights for agricultural purposes were recorded in 1861. By 1876, South Park was known as one of the principal hay-producing regions of the state.

In 1859, gold was discovered in Tarryall Creek and the rush was on. Hoards of gold-seekers spilled into the Park. Mining camps sprang up in every gulch and gulley. Soon the hills were dotted with towns bearing such colorful names as Tarryall, Buckskin Joe, Eureka, Horseshoe, and Mudsill.

Latecomers to the Tarryall diggings found themselves locked out. Disgruntled, they referred to the place as "Graball" and moved to the junction of Beaver Creek and the South Platte. They called their camp Fair Play and vowed to offer the same in good measure to all comers. The camp prospered, but soon the lone prospectors' stakes gave way to larger and more stable placer and hard-rock mining operations, which flourished for the next thirty years.

The South Park City Museum is an outdoor museum representing a Colorado mining town between 1870 and 1900. Thirty-two authentic buildings along with a wide variety of up to 60,000 authentic artifacts inside portray most of the economic and social aspects of Boom-Town life.

Booming towns in South Park were dependent on towns such as Denver and Canon City for food and tools. The gold and silver had to be shipped back to these centers. Wagon roads, and later, narrow gauge railroads, were built to accommodate the businessmen and miners. South Park, at one time, was served by three railroads: The Denver, South Park and Pacific; Colorado and Southern; and the Colorado Midland.

Professionally trained people came to South Park before 1900 to provide medical and educational services. As the community became more settled, skilled services such as carpentry and blacksmithing were needed to build houses and repair equipment. Social and fraternal organizations were a major part of many residents' lives. Other recreational outlets were provided by dance halls, saloons, and gambling houses of which "Rache's Place" is representative.

The log, batten, clapboard and stone buildings of the South Park City Museum illustrate the professions, trades, and industries that contributed to a 19th century mining town in Colorado and the romance of a by-gone era.

Main Street
South Park City, Colorado

Pioneer Home
Original Site

Kitchen Range, Pioneer Home
Original Site

Kitchen Table, Homestead House
Leavick, Colorado

Parlor Stove, Pioneer Home
Original Site

Pioneer Candlestick, Stage Stop

Kitchen Sink, Pioneer Home
Original Site

Wood Stove, Assay Office
London Mine Co.

Wash House, Garo Cabin
Garo, Colorado
c. 1895

Back Bar, Rache's Place
Alma, Colorado

Gambling Room Stove, Rache's Place
Alma, Colorado

Schoolhouse
Garo, Colorado
c. 1879

School Room
Garo, Colorado
c. 1879

Table & Chair, J.A. Merriam Drug Store
Alma, Colorado

Old Grinding Wheel Frame

Pitch Fork, Livery Stable
Fairplay, Colorado

Stage Barn
Mosquito Pass, Colorado

Window & Flowers, Pioneer Home
Original Site

Main Street
South Park City, Colorado

Window Reflections, Homestead House
Leavick, Colorado

Water Bucket, Homestead House
Leavick, Colorado

Wash Basin, Barber Shop
Fairplay, Colorado
c. 1870

Barber Shop
Fairplay, Colorado
c. 1870

Simpkins General Store
Dudley, Colorado

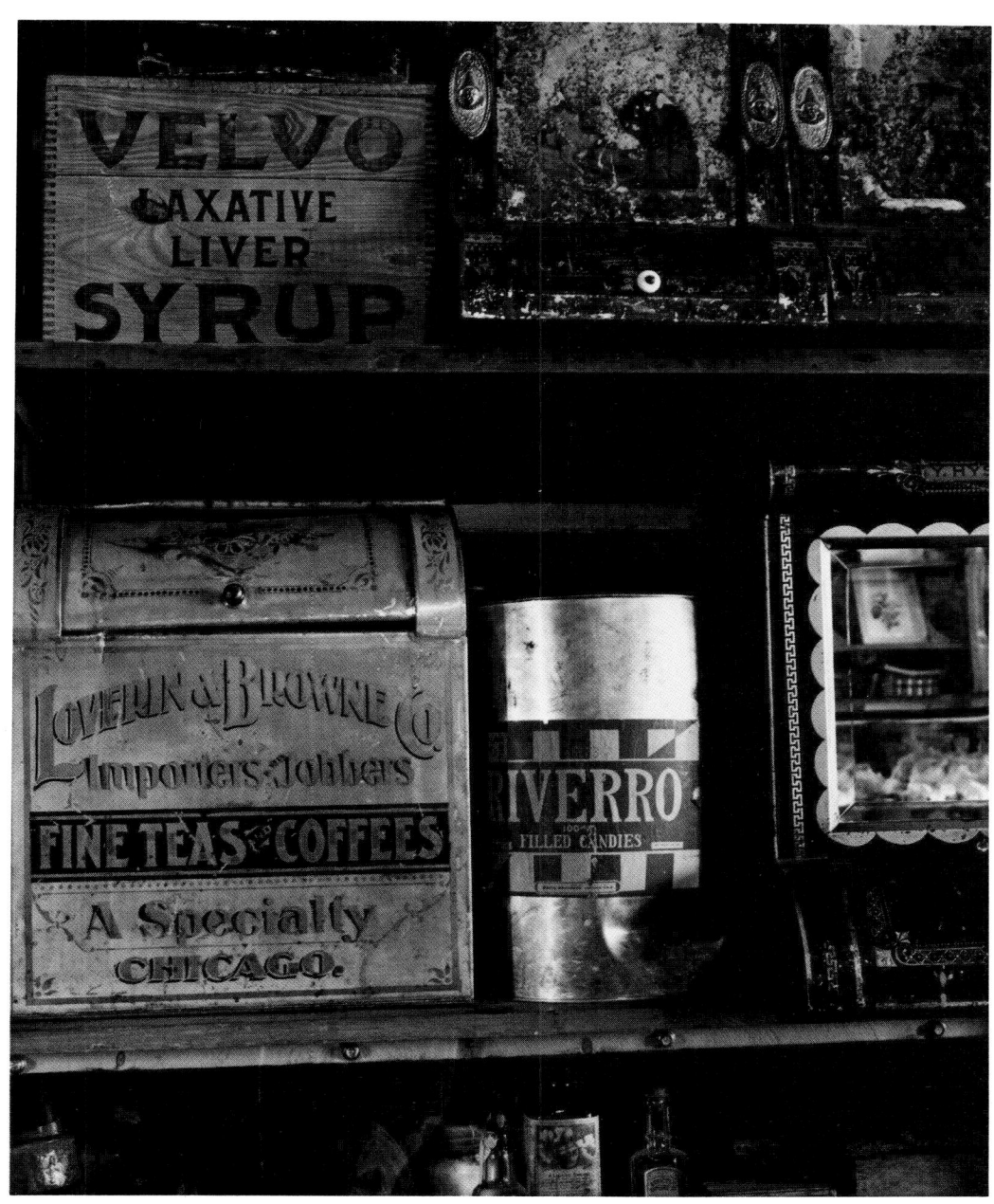

General Merchandise, Simpkins General Store
Dudley, Colorado

Drugs & Sundries, J.A. Merriam Drug Store
Alma, Colorado

Entrance Door, Bank of Alma
Alma, Colorado
c. 1870

Counter, J.A. Merriam Drug Store
Alma, Colorado

Chair & Stove, Simpkins General Store
Dudley, Colorado

Stage Coach Inn
Mosquito Pass, Colorado
c. 1879

Implements, Stage Barn
Mosquito Pass, Colorado

Butter Churn, Homestead House
Leavick, Colorado

Bedroom Door, Homestead House
Leavick, Colorado

Rache's Place
Alma, Colorado

Window & Curtains, Doctor's Office

Anvil & Chain, Hoffman Brothers Blacksmith Shop
Leavick, Colorado

Hoffman Brothers Blacksmith Shop
Leavick, Colorado

Telegrapher's Desk, South Park City Depot
South Park City, Colorado

Station Platform, South Park City Depot
South Park City, Colorado

Broken Window, Mayer House
Original Site

Leonard Summer Saloon
Original Site
c. 1879

Front Door, Mayer House
Original Site

John L. Dyer Memorial Chapel
Fairplay, Colorado

Dining Room Table, Pioneer Home
Original Site

Kitchen Range, Homestead House
Leavick, Colorado

Stove, Park County Court House
Buckskin Joe, Colorado
c. 1862

Street Scene, South Park City
South Park City, Colorado

Pioneer Bay Window, Homestead House
Leavick, Colorado

Back Door, Doctor's Office

Wagon, Stage Barn
Mosquito Pass, Colorado

Kitchen Window, Pioneer Home
Original Site

Gallows Frame, Phillips Mine
Buckskin Joe, Colorado

Mine Car
Original Location Unknown

Bellows & Tongs, Hoffman Brothers Blacksmith Shop
Leavick, Colorado

Narrow Gauge Locomotive, 1914 Porter Mogul No. 6

Sewing Machine, Homestead House
Leavick, Colorado

Clerk's Desk, Park County Court House
Buckskin Joe, Colorado

Drying Herbs, Homestead House
Leavick, Colorado

Equipment Graveyard, Blacksmith Shop

Work Table, Assay Office
London Mine Company
c. 1890

Razors & Hair Tonic, Barber Shop
Fairplay, Colorado
c. 1870

Coffee Grinder, Simpkins General Store
Dudley, Colorado

Window Images, Homestead House
Leavick, Colorado

Author's Note

The photographs in this book of South Park City Museum are from a collection of prints obtained over a four year period.

Natural available light was the only illumination light source; fill-in light was not utilized nor were bounce light reflectors.

A spotmeter was utilized particularly on the interior photographs to ensure the negative exposure would provide a *Zone III* placement of the dark shadow areas where detail was desired. Panatomic-X professional film exposed at ASA 48 was used in the 6x7 cm format negative size.

The film was tank processed in *Rodinal* developer 14 minutes at 72 degrees F. with a 1:80 dilution. The prints for reproduction were made on *Ilfospeed* Multigrade II glossy paper developed for one minute in *Dektol* diluted 1:2.

The prints were made with an enlarger modified with a cold light head. Print manipulation was utilized in the majority of photographs. Photographs of building interiors required dodging, and window areas particularly, required burning in.

Frank A. Cechner